Pebble® Plus

Investigate the Seasons

# Let's Look at Winter

Revised Edition

Sarah L Schuette

raintree
a Capstone company — publishers for children

Raintree is an imprint of Capstone Global Library Limited, a company incorporated in England and Wales having its registered office at 264 Banbury Road, Oxford, OX2 7DY – Registered company number: 6695582

www.raintree.co.uk
myorders@raintree.co.uk

Text © Capstone Global Library Limited 2018

**Editorial credits**
Sarah Bennett, designer; Tracy Cummins, media researcher, Laura Manthe, production specialist

**Photo credits**
Shutterstock: Africa Studio, 5, Bakusova, 19, Dieter Hawlan, 1, FotoRequest, Cover, Jeff Thrower, 17, Jim Cumming, 13, Khomulo Anna, 3, Liubou Yasiukovich, Cover Design Element, Marina Zezelina, 9, Ondrej Prosicky, 15, Peter Wey, 21, SnvvSnvvSnvv, 7, tim elliott, 11

Printed and bound in India

ISBN 978 1 4747 5657 0
22 21 20 19 18
10 9 8 7 6 5 4 3 2 1

**British Library Cataloguing in Publication Data**
A full catalogue record for this book is available from the British Library.

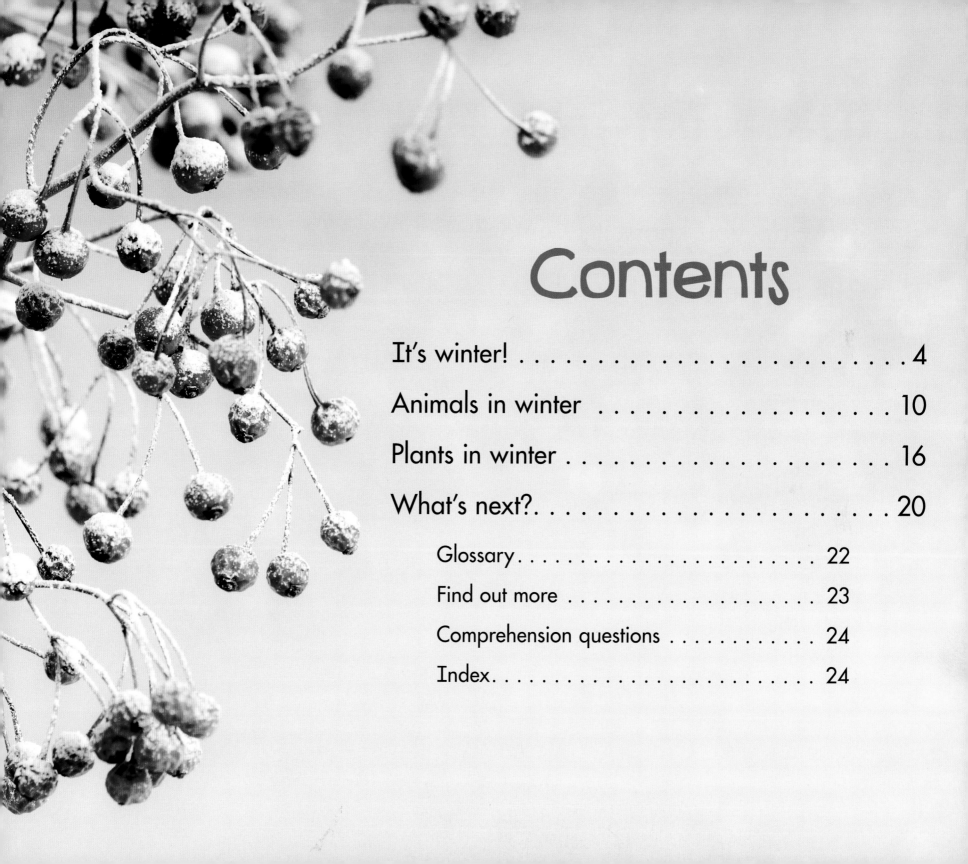

# Contents

# It's winter!

How do you know it's winter?

The temperature is cold.

The ground hardens.

Water freezes.

When snow falls,

it covers everything.

The sun rises later
in the morning.
Winter days are
the shortest of the year.

9

# Animals in winter

What do animals do

in winter?

Deer search for food

under the snow.

Some brown rabbits turn white.

Now their fur blends in

with the snow.

Owls sit in snowy trees.

They stay

for the whole winter.

Some birds migrate.

# Plants in winter

What happens

to plants in winter?

They do not grow.

Many plants look bare

and brown.

Evergreen trees stay green.

They keep their needles

all year round.

19

# What's next?

The temperature gets warmer.

Winter is over.

What season is next?

# Glossary

**bare**  not covered

**evergreen**  tree or bush that has green needles all year long

**freeze**  become solid or icy at a very low temperature

**migrate**  move from one place to another when seasons change

**needle**  sharp, green leaf on an evergreen tree

**season**  one of the four parts of the year; winter, spring, summer and autumn are seasons

**temperature**  measure of how hot or cold something is

# Find out more

## Books

*The Seasons* (Our Special World), Liz Lennon (Franklin Watts, 2016)

*What Can You See in Winter?* (Seasons), Sian Smith (Raintree, 2014)

*Winter* (Seasons), Stephanie Turnbull (Franklin Watts, 2015)

## Websites

www.bbc.co.uk/education/clips/zg9d6sg
Discover how winter weather affects animals and plants.

www.dkfindout.com/uk/earth/seasons
Find out more about the seasons on this website.

# Comprehension questions

1. How does white fur help some rabbits in winter?

2. What happens to the days in winter?

3. Describe what you like to do in winter.

# Index